Diplodocus

Written by Ron Wilson
Illustrated by Doreen Edwards

Library of Congress Cataloging in Publication Data

Wilson, Ron, 1941-
  Diplodocus.

  (The New dinosaur library)
  Summary: An introduction to the dinosaur known as Diplodocus, the longest land animal ever to live on the earth.
    1. Diplodocus—Juvenile literature.   [1. Diplodocus.
2. Dinosaurs]   I. Title.
QE862.S3W55   1984   567.9'7   84-8379
ISBN 0-86592-202-0

Rourke Enterprises, Inc.
Vero Beach, FL 32964

Diplodocus

Pteranodon

Woolly Mammoth

Diplodocus

Allosaurus

Hypsilophodon

Ichthyosaurus

The herd of Diplodocus had grown large. There had always been enough food for all. Each year the youngsters had stayed with the herd. Now things were different. Food had become scarce. Neither old nor young Diplodocus had enough to eat.

Some older members of the herd guarded the little food which was left. They rationed it out carefully. The creatures were allowed to feed early before the sun came up. Then they sought the meager shelter of the bare stems of one of the old trees. The Diplodocus had other problems. They had to protect their food from other plant eaters like Brontosaurus and Brachiosaurus.

Several older members of the herd were on duty guarding the plants when they were disturbed by a noise behind them. There were cracking branches and a general rumpus. The Diplodocus let out their customary warning call.

The advance continued. Large shapes appeared in the undergrowth all around. Allosaurus had appeared on all sides. The Diplodocus knew what this meant. They let forth cries for help as the intruders moved closer. The shrieks from the startled Diplodocus spread far and wide. Some herd members were sleeping; others resting. It was some time before the terrified cries reached all the members.

The younger Diplodocus had never been summoned like this before. As they saw other members of the herd move they followed them. Soon dozens of old and young were coming from all directions. Unceasing cries for help still came thick and fast from somewhere among the mass of dying vegetation.

The first arrivals saw strange and unfamiliar
shapes in front of them. They stopped in their tracks.
Most had never come across this situation before. They
had watched single members of the herd being attacked.
They had never seen so many large creatures. Panic
cries came from the Diplodocus guarding the food
supply. As other Diplodocus arrived at the scene of
activity they too slowly came to a halt. The Allosaurus
remained immobile too. The herd of Diplodocus was
not sure what the next move was.

The cries ceased. Diplodocus and their enemies
faced each other. The silence was intense. The quiet was
broken somewhere in the distance as a Brachiosaurus
called loudly to its mates.

Then, without any kind of signal the Allosaurus
advanced. They charged toward the Diplodocus
guarding the trees. For a moment there was utter
confusion. The old Diplodocus stood their ground,
letting out cries of anguish. The rest of the herd seemed
uncertain. Some stayed where they were; others backed
away.

The cries turned to terror as the Allosaurus attacked. Sharp teeth and claws sank into the Diplodocus' leathery skins. There was no hope. The old Diplodocus were no match for their attackers.

Each of the onlookers realized this. A few stayed to watch. Most fled away into the withered vegetation, their long necks poking out from the horsetails and ferns.

The herd split up. Some groups went one way; some another. Each continued on their slow lumbering way with hardly a backward glance. Normally the Diplodocus didn't have to move far. Today was different. If they were going to survive they would have to go a long way away. Instinct told them that once the Allosaurus had finished off the old Diplodocus they would look for other members of the herd.

Doreen
Edmond

They plodded clumsily on their way. In their haste they scattered numbers of small mammals feeding on the ground. A group of younger Diplodocus stayed together. A young female stopped for breath. She had never been so far in her life. She called out. It was a call for help. Most of them didn't seem to hear her call and continued on their way.

However, one young male Diplodocus did stop. He turned around to gaze at the frightened creature. He moved toward her, glad to help one of his kind.

They communicated, and the young male Diplodocus was soon aware of the female's problems. As they rested the young dinosaur was ever on the alert for danger.

After a while they moved forward slowly. Both were hungry. The Diplodocus searched until they found a few shrivelled leaves. They shared them. The older of the two made sure that the younger one had food to eat.

The male Diplodocus didn't recognize the area. There were no landmarks that he knew. The juvenile Diplodocus sensed a note of alarm in the older male's manner. She wasn't sure what it meant.

The two dinosaurs trudged slowly onward. The male paused now and then to try and get a bearing. He made continuous calls, listening anxiously for a reply. There was none. He had never been alone on his own before and fear overcame him.

In unfamiliar territory he was ever on the lookout for enemies, the earlier events were still vivid in his memory.

With the sun high overhead it was very hot. The male Diplodocus signalled to his female companion that they must soon try and find shelter. They were hungry and thirsty, conscious of the hot sun beating down on their leathery skins.

Suddenly a short distance in front of them, the older Diplodocus saw a rock. He approached it with caution. A small lizard scampered away into the undergrowth and startled him.

He indicated to the female Diplodocus to stay where she was. He thoroughly surveyed the rock, but there was no sign of life. He turned to the female Diplodocus, urging her to come toward the overhanging ledge. With room for both to shelter they stood very still, glad of time to rest.

Eventually the temperature dropped, and the two
hungry creatures moved off. The male Diplodocus led
the way. They searched every bush for food. They
found a leaf here and there and even nibbled at the
rough branches.

The older Diplodocus sniffed the air. Suddenly,
he caught the smell of conifers which drifted toward his
nostrils. He headed eagerly in the direction of the scent,
moving more quickly than he had done since escaping
from the Allosaurus. The female stayed close behind.
The male's pace quickened, the female finding it
difficult to keep up.

In front of them a whole plantation of lush vegetation came into view. Both creatures ate more than their fill and then wandered lazily to a nearby rock to rest.

The male dinosaur was awakened by faint sounds. He recognized them. They were from his own kind. He woke his younger companion.

Both creatures called back in unison. Soon the area was echoing with the sounds of many Diplodocus. After wandering far and wide they had all arrived in the same place.

There was plenty of food for all in the area which the young dinosaurs had found first.

Interesting facts about . . .
Diplodocus

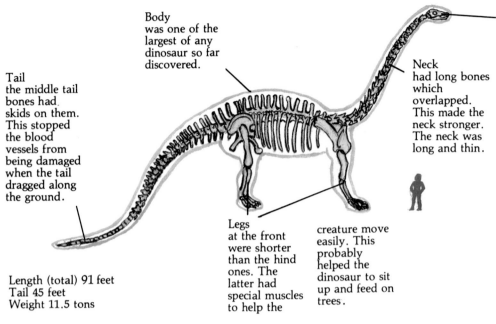

Tail
the middle tail bones had skids on them. This stopped the blood vessels from being damaged when the tail dragged along the ground.

Body
was one of the largest of any dinosaur so far discovered.

Neck
had long bones which overlapped. This made the neck stronger. The neck was long and thin.

Head
was small with the brain the size of a kitten's. There were small, thin teeth only in the front part of the jaws. There was a small hole above the eyes. This was the nostril.

Legs
at the front were shorter than the hind ones. The latter had special muscles to help the creature move easily. This probably helped the dinosaur to sit up and feed on trees.

Length (total) 91 feet
Tail 45 feet
Weight 11.5 tons

The skeleton of Diplodocus compared in size to a human

Double beam
Diplodocus means "double beam". It belongs to a group of dinosaurs called Sauropods. These were the longest land animals ever to live on the earth. The only animal which ever grew any bigger was the blue whale.

Diplodocus had a very small head at the end of a long neck. This neck was about 26 feet in length. At the other end of the body was a whip-like tail, which was about 45 feet 6 inches long. Altogether the creature was about 91 feet in length. It probably weighed between 10 and 15 tons. As we said, Diplodocus was the longest creature ever to walk the earth. However, it wasn't the heaviest. Brontosaurus (which is known as Apatosaurus) weighed as much as 30 tons. This is five times the weight of a modern elephant.

Diplodocus had light bones
The backbone of Diplodocus was very light. Their bones were hollowed out. In spite of this it was still a very heavy creature. Its leg bones were solid to support its heavy weight.

Where did Diplodocus live?
At one time scientists thought that Diplodocus must have lived in water. Nowadays people have changed their minds. They think the creature lived in the swampy areas. They probably used their long necks to take leaves from high up on trees.

Why did scientists think Diplodocus lived in water?
Scientists believed the dinosaur lived in water because the creature had such small legs. These would not have held them up on land. Water is more buoyant and would support the creature more easily. When scientists first looked at the teeth of the Sauropods, including Diplodocus, they thought they were weak. This suggested to them that they could only deal with very soft plants like seaweeds. Soft plants grew in water.

Further studies on the teeth showed that they were not weak as they first thought. Evidently, Diplodocus ate hard plants. This was what caused their teeth to wear down.

Comparing Diplodocus to other water animals
Scientists have compared Diplodocus to other water animals. They have found that the shapes of the bodies of Sauropods are different. Most water animals have bullet-shaped bodies which help them move through the water more easily. They also have short necks. The feet of Diplodocus wouldn't have been much use in muddy conditions. They didn't spread out far enough. The creature would have gotten stuck in the mud.

Why Diplodocus was probably a land animal

All these are good reasons for thinking that Diplodocus was a land animal. However, there is one other reason. The weight of water pressing on the dinosaur's chest and lungs would have stopped it from breathing properly.

Dinosaur eggs

The Sauropods were egglaying creatures like the other dinosaurs. Perhaps you would expect a creature as large as Diplodocus to lay a large egg. Actually, the female laid quite a small one. Many dinosaur eggs have been found. They were roundish in shape and probably about 10 inches in length.

When did Diplodocus live?

Diplodocus roamed the earth about 150 million years ago. This was during the Jurassic period. The age of Dinosaurs went from the Triassic (235 million years ago) to the Cretaceous (65 million years ago). The Jurassic was the middle one of these three periods.

Enemies of Diplodocus

There were many plant eating dinosaurs which lived at the same time as Diplodocus. These included Brachiosaurus and Brontosaurus. There were also large, ferocious flesh eating dinosaurs. These included Allosaurus, which was the largest. An agile Diplodocus, would probably not have been attacked by Allosaurus. In fact, the young and old probably were.

Things to do

Make a mobile. Cut out dinosaur shapes. Use the creatures shown in this book for ideas. Hang your models from a coat hanger using cotton.

See if you can discover stories about monsters which might look rather like Diplodocus.

Make a model of a scene from the book. You will need a cardboard box. Cut out the front. Make plants from paper and card. Make dinosaur models from plastic or other modelling material. Make a small theater using the idea above. You could then make various scenes like those in the book. Cut out model dinosaurs and perform your story.

Try and discover as many other Sauropods as you can. Compare their way of life.

Make a drawing of Diplodocus. Then make drawings of some of the everyday things around you. Perhaps you could use a sofa, a car, a chair and so on. Draw everything to scale. Paste your Diplodocus on a sheet of paper. Then arrange your other items around his picture. You will be able to see how big he was compared with some of the things which you know. Perhaps you might like to add a scale drawing of your home as well.

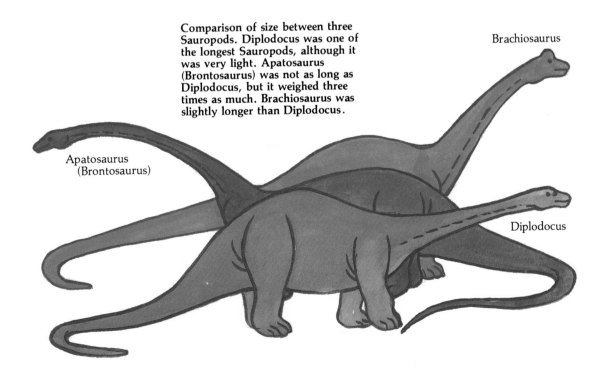

Comparison of size between three Sauropods. Diplodocus was one of the longest Sauropods, although it was very light. Apatosaurus (Brontosaurus) was not as long as Diplodocus, but it weighed three times as much. Brachiosaurus was slightly longer than Diplodocus.

Brachiosaurus

Apatosaurus (Brontosaurus)

Diplodocus